The Way I See Things

A Collection of Contemporary Poetry

ADOLFO RUDY GELSI

Copyright © 2023 Adolfo Rudy Gelsi.

All rights reserved. No part of this book may be reproduced, stored, or transmitted by any means—whether auditory, graphic, mechanical, or electronic—without written permission of both publisher and author, except in the case of brief excerpts used in critical articles and reviews. Unauthorized reproduction of any part of this work is illegal and is punishable by law.

ISBN: 979-8-88640-935-2 (sc)
ISBN: 979-8-88640-936-9 (hc)
ISBN: 979-8-88640-937-6 (e)

Because of the dynamic nature of the Internet, any web addresses or links contained in this book may have changed since publication and may no longer be valid. The views expressed in this work are solely those of the author and do not necessarily reflect the views of the publisher, and the publisher hereby disclaims any responsibility for them.

One Galleria Blvd., Suite 1900, Metairie, LA 70001
1-888-421-2397

Contents

1. Rose (My Town) 3
2. The Emigrant 4
3. Charlatan Laws 5
4. I am a Number 6
5. Path of Life 7
6. Dream of Freedom 8
7. Your Shadow 9
8. Lost World 10
9. The Naked Picture 11
10. My Fault Now 12
11. Message to No One 13
12. Freedom 14
13. Telling It Like It Is 15
14. Who Stole my Heart 16
15. Don't Stand Aside 17
16. A Tree and A Flower 18
17. The Truth About Me 19
18. White Flower 21
19. Rain 22
20. The Shadow 23
21. Supreme I Am 24
22. A Friend 26
23. Death is Near 27
24. Homeless 28
25. The Procession 29
26. Departure 31
27. An Angel in the Family 32
28. Two Dark Souls 33

29. Satisfaction is the Word 35
30. Snowing 36
31. Tears of Love 37
32. Hope 38
33. Going to War 39
34. We: John, Carol and Lauren 41
35. Ready to Die 42
36. Revenge 43
37. The Beggar 44
38. Into Eternity 46
39. Just Thinking 47
40. Leave God Alone 49
41. Lost Behind a Dream 50
42. Never Make It 51
43. Awake Me 52
44. Me and the World 53
45. Reservations in this World 54
46. Wondering 55
47. Going over the Line 56
48. Today's World 57
49. My Child 58
50. Waiting 59
51. The Call 60
52. What I can Say 61
53. Dark Room 62
54. Ghosts at the Beardsley Park 63
55. The Stranger 64
56. Littleton (New Hampshire) 65
57. Son of the Past Love 66
58. Good Morning to All 67
59. Searching 68
60. You Are 69

61.	Her Memory	70
62.	That Name	71
63.	How Lucky I Am	72
64.	Dreams are Real	73
65.	You Talking	74
66.	Calling	75
67.	Blind Vision	76
68.	The Man on the Hill	77
69.	My Son One Day	78
70.	Thoughtful	79
71.	To my Mother's Memories	80
72.	Women Coming and Going	81
73.	No Sense Talking	82
74.	My Star is Here	83
75.	Midnight in the Woods of New Hampshire	84
76.	Nothing Left	86
77.	Divine Love	87
78.	Contemporary	88
79.	The Fallen Oak	89
80.	Show in the Street	90
81.	My House	91
82.	Ideas	92
83.	Here to Stay	93
84.	Leave me Alone	94
85.	Orphan Baby Boy	95
86.	Leaving Earth	96
87.	I Am	97
88.	Missing Time	98
89.	Nature	99
90.	Fall is Here	100
91.	The News	101
92.	One Night Stand	102

93. Today's Young Generation 103
94. A Fact of Reality 104
95. A Gift for You 105
96. World, New Beginning 106
97. You and Me 107
98. Do You Know Love 108
99. Infinite Thinking 109
100. The Story Goes On 110
101. Not Responsible Youth 111
102. Alone I Am Not 112
103. The Transvestite 113
104. Running for Happiness 114
105. My House in Winter Time 115
106. You my Ghost 116
107. The Upper Room 117
108. Unrestful Night 118
109. Talking Simplicit 119
110. I am the Soldier 120
111. I Live for Her 121
112. Vacationing 122
113. Nightingales on my Windowsill 123
114. Accused 124
115. The Way I see Things 125

My name is Adolfo Gelsi, known as Rudy to my friends. I was born in Italy in the small town of Rose in the province of Cosenza, a city with a history of barbarian assail, as the geographic position allows those who travel from the Mediterranean access to the main land. Calabria is the region where Rose is located, a beautiful land in any real sense of the world. The mountains are full of all kinds of vegetarian herbs with specific uses in the pharmaceutical field, the wild fruit in abundance for anyone to pick and bring home to jar for the winter. The sea has water so clean that you can admire the fine sand on the bottom and see the fish swimming. The beauty of my region is imprinted in my thoughts. Day after day the memory of what I left in my country keeps me thinking if living my life was made better in any sense of the word. I still keep the origins alive. The month of August 1970 is when my life changed. I had the opportunity to immigrate to America. At that time America was a country where people immigrated to have a better future not just for themselves, but also for their children. I was a twenty-two year old boy who, after graduating from college, with no future on hand tried very hard to make a career in the Italian Army. Two years had passed since my enlistment in the army, life wasn't all joy, but the city where I was located was beautiful. Verona, the city of Romeo and Juliet, so beautiful in any sense of the word . . . antique castle walls that tell the story of the city, streets made of stone where no cars were allowed to drive to keep the beauty of the eternal city. I loved to be there, but when a letter from the American Embassy came in the mail, my world changed. I had a month to decide my future, leave everything and get on the first plane to America or throw the letter in the garbage and pursue my career in the Italian Army. I wasn't selfish with my decision. I consulted with my superiors, especially my Capitan, a gentleman that still, today, 42 years later, we talk on the phone at least once a year. Also, there was another problem with my decision, how to confront my family, especially my mother. How would I tell her that I had a chance to go to America and have a better future? I had so little time to make up my mind. I asked for some time off from the Army, to go home and have a reunion with my entire family, the Capitan give me the permission for a week off, and told me that I was a lucky man to have the opportunity to go to America, and to do everything possible to convince my family to let me go, and have a better future, being in the Army was a good future, especially in regards to having whatever was necessary for a decent living, but nothing more. In America the Captain was telling me that I had more opportunities to do whatever I would like to. Maybe go back to school, or go to work in a factory and for sure I would make more money than I was making in the Italian Army. It wasn't easy to decide what to do, so I took the first train and went back home, where my family was waiting for me. At home everything was normal, no tears or long hugs, like something bad had happened. I knew I didn't have a lot of time at my disposal and that was the reason that after a nice dinner I informed my family of the opportunity that was presented to me to leave Italy and go to the United States of America. Of course my family didn't like the idea of me leaving all of them and departing to another part of the world, but it was up to me to convince them that my life would be better once I had established myself in the United States. It didn't take me long to convince them to let me go. In less than a month I was ready to leave Italy and go to the United States of America where dreams would come true. Writing a collection of poetry is one of my dreams. And the dream came true.

Rose (My Town)

In time memory erases visual encounter
The beauty of antique structure will disappear from my thoughts.
But the name remains the same
Rose (My Town)
Just the name could be interpreted as beautiful as can be.
A flower if you like an adjective if you please, a noun, a pronoun.
Or for instance the name of a beautiful girl.
In many ways I am personally elated.
But the name remains the same
Rose (My Town)
The old castle being as King for generations.
The antique church where once assembled the faithful,
And how I can forget the fountain on the small square Gaetano Argento
With that limpid water so fresh and tasteful
That we, as kids lined up with the hand as a cup
To quench our thirst after a soccer game of three hours or
more at the Cipitti.
The very tiny streets built by calloused hands one stone after another
Carried from the ravine on top of the head.
From our ancestors,
Houses made of clay decorated with beautiful wild plants that grow on their own.
How can I get my memory back to restore that visual existence of my town?
There is where I was born. There is where my youth is.
When alone in the solitude of the White Mountains of New Hampshire
My memory and thoughts take my heart there where I extend my hand.

The Emigrant

Born in a small town
Where life wasn't easy as he remembers
Driven out from the living hell
He knew that he would become an emigrant.
It wasn't right, emotionally torn
To find a place to have him embrace
A peasant he was with racial divides
In Religious beliefs to overcome his grief
The Emigrant
Lived in a place where language was a stranger
Forbidden to understand what words really meant.
Celebrating freedom with hard work and tears
For a generation of new creations.
Was the ethic of a better place
Remembering where he came from
Torn and abused in a strange country.
Time has come to go back home
Where his family is still there working the land.
No more strange words or ethics to follow
He is home now in the small town
Where his memory returns in time
When as a youth he left his land
To become an emigrant.

Charlatan Laws

At night when the darkness obscures the essence of life
I stand breathing in the middle of nowhere
Scrutinizing the galaxies with thoughts of mortal concepts
Growing in to my weak mind to see my soul flowing into the inner celestial circle
Somewhere freedom thrives in the cosmic skies
And no laws of charlatan humans will prevail
Through the celestial galaxies pure mysteries will be revealed.
To the one that stands and knows that the gift of creation
Is far from the dark planet beneath.
Charlatan Human.
You impose the laws making sure that your figure arises
Don't wait for me in the daylight
When you again show your supreme stance
Destroying the concept of real life
I forever escape from your writing
Find refuge through the obscure essentials of life
Hoping to rise into the freedom of celestial galaxies
Leaving the laws of the charlatans to sway supreme
The planet beneath.
Waiting from the above seeing that the polluted soil
Will be filled with charlatan human decay
Where once we enjoyed the ride of a lifetime.

I am a Number

What weight my death will have in this world
When I never give anything in reward
Obstinate silence at my literary work to which
No one ever gives back an answer will remain
In a dumb waiter full of dust from time well past
In this world unresponsive I emerge accustomed
To living my ways I will remain restrained
One more time I ask for support hoping that
Someone will hear and give me a stroke of luck
I have no family to dedicate my thoughts
The daily dilemma takes me far away from reality
I am a number
My catholic name forgotten
My headstone is there in the dirt of this polluted earth
That eventually will vanish in time
Oh! You supreme what good deed flourishes
Conceiving all as equal
And you all honorably do not have the persuading
Thoughts to be dissimilar
Because when your time comes
You too will be six feet under
For a week or two tears will be shared
You will remembered and status be spoken
But at the end, no one will recall
Because even you are just a number.

Path of Life

Time doesn't always erase
The path of life
Tears and distress plague your heart
Wrinkles show your age
I search for a solution
No smile, no gaze, silence all
An act to feel in my heart
If I was a writer
I would write a book
Telling anyone about it
The path of life
Having a true said to reach an act
Never hide the pain under a nasty smile
Praying at the high sky to hear me
Never ask to hide the truth
Under a lying surface
Path of life
I would like to change life
Reborn again and start
The sacrifice of being rejuvenated
Isn't easy to follow obscure avenues
That make you fall
No substance to hold on
Mind and body will someday arise.

Dream of Freedom

Nights divide days
In the hope that the light of a new sunrise
Will bring alert smiles
Dreams of freedom
Lately vanish into obscure thoughts
Freedom for all has been trampled for so many years
Where?
Tell me now before I go insane
I got to extend my dream
Flying into the high sky to find my freedom
Where are the values favorable to grow into life
I have been blinded from shining arsenals
That dictate statements of fake power
Give me back my freedom
To enjoy the steps of nature
Give me the happiness taken away
By you supreme commander of darkness
I was dreaming of spring days
Breathing the freshness emanating from fields of flowers
I was dreaming of summer days
Warmed by golden rays shooting from blue skies
I was dreaming of fall days
Seeing foliage flying around me
Expressing freedom of landing
I was dreaming of winter days
Bright white mountains cleaning the air
Polluted from the chaos of civilization
The dreams vanish into wakeful nights
I repose in a bed of tears of deprived freedom
This is a life of uncertain future
Dreams of freedom
Are only tears on wakeful nights.

Your Shadow

There isn't an hour of the day
That I don't search for your smile
Far from my eager desire
That makes my heart ache
The memory of dreaming thoughts
Rising above my mental power
From faraway lands
To the green mountains of a small town
Lost forever in visions past
The churches and monuments
Are memories of your smile.
Enlightened by a vision of your face
Oceans of blue water divide our souls
I cry but you can't hear
Your shadow turns sadness into love
And I sail into your heart
Speaking my past language
Singing love and harmony for you
Your shadow
Into eternal white at the summit of the mountains
And the always green valley
Where pure water runs downhill
Memories never die
Awaking the sense of love making
In a strange nestling from another land of pleasure
The beauty that never satisfies
Hold me in your thoughts as I am away
At my death restfully pose my body into the cold ground
Your tears penetrate the soil
To warm my mortal remains.

Lost World

Lost world in a crater of dirt
Where breathing is difficult
And darkens every day of our living
Salt water of polluted sea
Washes the alarming impurities
That suffocate mountains and hills
Let us excavate a wild retreat
To save our souls
Dying on the surface of this lurid planet
Where hypocrisy reigns
In the hand of the justice
Where is it?
The fire to sterilize the polluted sand
Needed to rub out minds full of sin
Awaking from a dream of time lost
Where sour fumes rise over dry hills
And flowers grow covering the infected site
The sun hardly gives a smile
The water flows down to kill
And terrestrial disasters can be viewed
From skies of this lost world
Wet chicks from a lava of blood
Run from shut eyes
Tired of the devastation they encounter
In this short stay
Let's all try one more awakening
Maybe see the last smile
Or breathe some fresh fragrance
Where once polluted soil was our carpet
As we walked upon it
With our cancerous feet.

The Naked Picture

In the squalor of the dark room
Where I spend my existence
I have a naked picture
Hung on the wall
The beautiful eyes follow me
From every angle
The pure face adorned with rose lips
Smiling at every turn I take
An old chair full of dust
Is where I sit to admire
The naked picture.
It isn't real, it is just a game
That controls my mind.
What's going on my strained body implies
I am going insane
Closing my eyes to ease the pain
Repeating to myself wake up
Face reality
There isn't anything to see
The naked picture
Staring at my strained soul
Talking on sight
So many sins we have committed
All through the years we have given
Every second, minute and hour
Forming a day and a night
Where sweat washes our bodies, all gone now.
Wrinkles cover our bodies
What once was beautiful energy
The naked picture
Remains pure in time
Smiling, looking, saying goodbye.

My Fault Now

Maybe she isn't so guilty
Maybe she isn't so wrong
Maybe I should never have acted the way I did
Maybe that is the reason
That everything went wrong
My fault now
That I understand why
An easy life full of expectations
This is what I was living for
Joyful times from that angel face
Before the truth rose from under lies
I wasn't that saint to give up all
Stop living my life the way I know
My fault now
If her smile is miles away
No tears or words can repair
The evil of wakeful nights
Where abandoned into sinister sins
Thoughts of her were joys of the past
My fault now
If a satisfying future is out of reach
Beyond repair my sins stand
She isn't so guilty she isn't so wrong
To turn away from a story
That finally I understood.

Message to No One

Whereabouts, unknowing, lost

No one knows where

In the middle of dry dirt, and wet sky

There isn't anything I can do

Wondering if someone will find me

I am a ghost and the days are dark

From time past how I get here

Walking for miles destination unknown

It is a hopeless situation, population zero

Time that I waste

To find someone and send a message

I lay in the dry dirt makes no sense

My waiting is gloomy

Still in the dark I fight to breathe

In a senseless thought

I want to send a message

Truly just a message

Just be elsewhere, far from a polluted population

With my eyes shut, thinking

Who can hear my message?

Maybe they are all deceased from a virus

Those I called the new generation

I start now screaming

Let me be here

In the middle of nowhere eyes wide open

Nobody hears what I have to say

Message to no one

I will stand as a ghost with my thoughts

Where darkness is falling

And is here to stay.

Freedom

Go free
Go free into the desert castle
Where you left your youth
In that castle on top the world
Go free
Give light to the dark room
Where your body once was king
Where your body once was splendor.
In the darkness around
Think free
Think free like a big river
That washes away all the sins
Think free like the crystal water
That I never will see
Blind from darkness
I am in the captivity of imagination
And you know it
I am in captivity in this world
Without care and love
And you know it
Go free!
Go free to give life to life
Go free
To revive my soul with light
From the obscure walls
Let me see the light again
Let me reach into your soul
Into the new universe and be free

Telling It Like It Is

What keeps me awake at night, and why
I ask
What breaks my heart
To make me so sad and cry
I said a Prayer to never turn my back
And harden my ways of thinking
Or try to frighten credent souls
The evil is among us
Should never forget that
Telling it like it is
So everyone can hear me
Screaming at the world
With anger and grief
To make dry eyes cry
Telling it like it is
Never shut your vision to pretend
What we see isn't real
I will I said, loud and clear
We live in a rotten and miserable world
I always talk about horror
That torments the souls inside
Telling it like it is
No one forgets breaking the ties
And silencing the binds
Never top anyone's ears
Or shut my mouth
I will tell the world about
How it is
No silent rumors between the speech
I won't run far or fast
Making lives secure
Telling the truth is my intent
For now to the end
Lies never will cross my lips
Telling it like it is.

Who Stole my Heart

There are locks on the door
Cross-bars on the windows
Chains stretching across the entries
Gates and fences on the inside
Protect me from what lurks outside
God knows
Who stole my heart?
Left an empty space
A cavity that no one can fill
Who is the one that took it,
Knowing that without it I can't live
Who takes away that organ?
So essential to the whole
Who is the one
That left your hollow body bone and skin.
Who is that thief?
Who stole my heart?
That took the key of a bright future
Who erased the smile from my face
And blinded the innocent light from my eyes
Who stole my heart?
Maybe no one, maybe I gave it away
If it is so
When will I get it back?
For now I will trust no one to return it
Who stole my heart?
Don't forget that moment in time
What trickster lurked
With no reason to apply
Just took my heart away, and killed.

Don't Stand Aside

Supreme and absolute
That gave birth to the universe
You that from above keep watching
Don't stand aside.
From the beginning
We mortals have sinned
It is a crime to you, Supreme
To the end there is no glory
Let your voice be heard
Don't stand aside.
You witnessed the end of the world
We poisoned the beauty that you created
Soil, flowers, trees
Air we can't breathe
Don't cry Supreme
Before the end you will testify
Don't stand aside.
What you saw with your own eyes
You've got to survive
Don't testify
Bring the salvation of the universe
Hold the planet in your hands
Fill our souls with joyful thoughts
Give us the wisdom to abide
The laws written from You Supreme
Look over us to not poison the beauty
Don't stand aside.
We need You now
Don't wait until we all die.

A Tree and A Flower

Nothing will give joy in this world
Even death will be in emptiness
Before you depart
Scared times from loneliness
Will be your companion
Don't cry, make sense of your living
Plant a tree, carve your name
Don't wait until tomorrow
It will be too late
For memories passed.
That tree will grow with loving thoughts
Left by you to us all
Leave a stand in this world
Remind us of your existence
Plant a flower in someone's heart
Give that flower a name
To be cherished as time passes
As seasons change that flower blooms
Reminding us of the emptiness left behind
Memories will never be erased
You will be remembered
Because the tree and the flower
Will keep your name alive.

The Truth About Me

At this stage of my life
I've done so many things
Putting your trust in me
I hope I don't let you down.
Give me a chance or I will cry
It has been a hard road to follow
Give me your hand and soul
I will take you down the right road
I've had a shaky start in life
In this country that isn't mine.
I say the truth
You all understand my rights
I am doing the best at this point
Although I've mostly walked in shadow.
I'm still searching for that light.
If you give me a chance
I am sure I will find it
I have to climb the stairs
Searching the top
Without stumbling down
I have to conquer hills
And not go down
I've got to do my best

No time to repent
Before I make any more promises
Before I have any regrets
Let me tell all about my past
All I've seen and all I have done
The truth about me
If I can live as if only love matters
As if redemption was in sight
As if I live honestly I will touch the sky
The earth's gravity has pulled me down
I've got to reconcile
To this world of mine
This is the truth of my life.

White Flower

I will never have white flowers for you
Just have intense patience and silent thoughts
I will cherish your beauty
Lighting the morning
I know the laws in this world
I will redeem the gloom and the dirt
For the love that I have
Is so special it's yours
I will obscure the light
To preserve you inside
My soul mate of this passing life
Can't forget the tears in your eyes
The silky touch that never dies
Joyous moments of our life
Where are the white flowers
For you to accept with pride
A stimulating site
Never looking back, it's a new light
So cherish the scent before they die
You and I and the white flowers

Rain

Over the river I see a light
Maybe is the light of my salvation
Rain
The water is so high
I don't think I will make it
I got to try, that light calls me
Hungry, tired and wet
The water rises
Rain
The whistling of the wind
Penetrating my bones, it is a blizzard
My shoes are broken water wets my feet
I got to go over the river
That light calls it seems near
Rain
I got to conquer the water
Hours rush on
I got no time
Rain
I am breathing the cold air of the night
Trembling, staggering
Trying to get courage
Looking at the sky
Seeing a star I can follow
I have to cross the river
Raise the flag for victory
Feel free and saved
Touching the light having faith
In a sunny tomorrow.
Still rain.

The Shadow

Day after day
That whispering voice obscures my thoughts
It is a shadow into my soul
That talks to me, saying
That love will never turn back
I fight that shadow
I don't believe what I hear
That whisper is a lie
Consuming my existence
I keep walking forward
No new adventures
The world is the same
I see what I believe
Not turning back to what I have
What it was, it still is
Nothing new at the horizon
The roses are still red
That red that covers your virgin soul
No love is left
No chance to do so
The meadow is still green
And will be for us to run through it
There is nothing new I got to go forward
I got to reach the finish line
Still believe in the dream of reality
The shadow is still there
Whispering what he knows about past love
Through the light my eyes don't see anything new
It is love and pain that I share
Thinking of the present
I awake
That is what I remember.

Supreme I Am

So you say

That my artful way of performing tricks

Indulges you to be mine

That strong elixir so sweet tasting

I drank a portion smiling at you

Was my trick, a way to conquer your body

Supreme I am

Bruising the soul of my loving mate

No one can heal the wounds

If wizards, princes, magic men and witches

Can see the rotten in me

The indifference of my soft touch

And sentiments evaporating through the nights

In the dark sky full of impurities

Supreme I am

If I still have the trust

To tear down the walls

To reach my next victim

My artful way of performing

Will always indulge any one to mate

I never throw my armor away

To remove the barricade

To forget the sins of my performances

I am a bandit in search of prey

With that gentle touch
Defending what I have conquered
With my artful way of performing
Your heart is mine
I stole it you said;
Send a cavalier army I reply
To take it away from me
Keep praying my sweet mate
Your soul is mine now and forever
Supreme I am
And I will say:
I don't know your name.

A Friend

An immortal friend you are
Always in my thoughts you will be
No past memory I will have
But a smile for a better future
At a new horizon I believe
The ocean divides us
But the brotherhood and open heart
Keeps us united
You are a friend
That the world dreams
And your name is not a shame
Dreaming the scene
Of joy and sorrow
I would like you near
A friend you are not
Brother to me in my heart and thoughts
Oh friend from a faraway land
Wait for me with open hands
One day not far
I will embrace you again
Because you are my immortal friend.

Death is Near

I see people of all ages dying
Along the road to nowhere
Searching for a dream that takes to insanity
In search of something that does not exist in this world
Wet nights from alcohol and drugs
Transformed into clouds
Smoke in the heart of the city
Swallows the civilization on the road
Cars bought with no credit
Gentle people stunned at the events
Lost in the sight of beliefs
My generation is dying
Why they camouflage with faith
Docile everlasting country of erotic events
Usually scared of political speech
Carrying the interest of dignity
Into the emptiness of hypocrisy
From whom we think is always right
And never wrong as he says
In the field of destruction
In the race of political affairs
Death is near
The new generation has to profess
Into this new world
Full of hope born into the future
They have no hands
A revolution without arms
Because we know and believe
That everyone will die
Waiting to rise again
As God did.

Homeless

She's crying on a corner of the street
Lying on reality is what best eases her mind
It's just a game, dying
When someone will find
She can't make it through the night
Keeps falling, hiding, and crying
Homeless
You get kicked when down
Tears calling all over town
A helping hand she needs now
It isn't a game she's playing
Nothing to say
Fire burns from deep inside
When a hand is giving
A heart longing, fear disappears
So in silence she stands
Waiting to fall again
Time will tell
Homeless
Day after day years go by
Still waiting for a miracle
To stop crying
Never realizing all the questions in her mind
An answer to life
Is waiting all over town.

The Procession

Narrow streets in front of us
Faithful jammed tight progressing slowly
No one has died
It is the Saint above the shoulders
Protecting the crowd
The Procession is alive
Can hear voices praying aloud
Bells toll playing tunes of joy
It is the Saint they salute looking at the sky
Open hearts smiling at all
The hot rays of the sun
Drops of sweat run down the spine
The joyful faces of children scattering around
The fountain on the corner
Holy water running
Quenches the thirsty mouths
Of the faithful creatures
The Procession
Of the beloved Saint progresses
To an unnamed street
I follow praying in silence
Can't sing
I pray that a Miracle will be granted

That the Saint hears my thoughts
Maybe He will.
At the square we arrive
Where the Saint will stand high
All the faithful watching eyes
Attracting kids and parents
Of all races joyful, playing
The stands full of goods
Smelling of food from far way countries
Purifying the air around
The procession stops
The Saint has arrived
Standing tall
With a watchful smile.

Departure

I am ready

The time has come to depart

Far away land waiting for my arrival

As an emigrant I will embrace

Joyous and sad moments of solitude

First time seeing the sea

Amazed by the beauty of the salty blue water

As teenager I left town

The shadow of green eyes

Follows my thoughts

Sun and moon don't look the same

As the fisherman watches over

He too is an emigrant

Knows what his heart wants

Sign of the Cross at every mile

The salt water of the sea became Holy

In mind the green mountains that I have left behind

Departure far away

Hot rays following us

Wishing good luck in a new land

For a hundred years greeting us strangers

The water always reminds us

Ways to go back in time

Dreams begin

Hard to find

Living in far way land

To keep in mind.

An Angel in the Family

Family is everything that we have

If an Angel isn't there

Nothing will prevail

The rancor and pain are less sour

If an Angel in the family we have

The women are angels to stay

Moms, sisters, wives are they

Angels care for family affairs

Suffering of days ending

With advise and care

Last, a kiss for the mothers

Who tell about life

Respect and love

Are teachings to stay

The soul never tires

Because of the faith

Of an Angel in the family.

Two Dark Souls

What an incredible night
Sweat dripping from our bodies
A glass full of dreams
Disgusting hair falling
Into my glass on the side of bed
Two dark souls motionless
I got to stop drinking
My lover's white hair covering the site
Strangely romantic it was
Two evil kids we were
Tears coming down innocent faces
Dreams flying
We will go to Heaven
No love there just smiling
The moon lights over the blue sea
I can't swim
I will die in the salt water
Hoping someone is there
I don't know what to do
Love is mindless of time
Give me two tickets to fly

Destination unknown
We will depart to a new obscure site
Tender lips, green eyes,
Kiss tasting of poison
This what we are
Two Dark souls
We again fall into sin
Don't be afraid always gentle
I will make you fly
To the stars
Tonight is special
I will carry you to the high light
Can't think of the past
The new future is there
The universe opening its arms
Waiting for us sinners
No white hair to fall
Pure fire keeps us warm.

Satisfaction is the Word

I want to live the way it is
If possible to the end
Now that I understand
The world around me
Interesting events
Holding principles of life
To never turn back to the dark side
Satisfaction is the word
Now that life smiles on me
No more visions of persistent turmoil
That is in the past, time erodes my soul
No more dreams of the world on fire
Giving me pleasure keeps me alive
Satisfaction is the word
Now that I find my way around
Moments of thinking of time lost
When living in the fast lane
Was the only resource
Aging put sense in my thoughts
Kindness I have for the surroundings
Nature, animals and gentile
I salute with overwhelming respect
Smiling at the new day that is born
I thank the dying moon
Say hello to the rising sun
At the beauty in front my eyes
Satisfaction is the word.

Snowing

Black smoke evaporating into the air
Burning old wood found in the field
Walls painted in black
From the old wood burning stove
Cracks on the old chimney
Incense my soul
Into thoughts of the past
I sit next to the frosted window
Where the cold glass shows
White beauty coming down
Snowing
The frozen grass once green
Patches of brown soil turning white
Naked trees sleeping
Waiting for the rays of the sun
To say good morning
Blowing beautiful
Purification is what to think about
Snowing
The cold light penetrating the frozen glass
Illuminating the black walls
Where a cloud of smoke
Finds its way through the ruptured structure
Snowing
The singing birds
Searching for a secure place
Keep me company in the desolation
Of the now frozen flat surroundings
As I keep burning.

Tears of Love

Even for us
There is a reason why we are here
If you hold me tight
I will soak your body with tears
I will cry until I let myself go dry
Tears of love
A man that lost his heart in the streets
Wandering in fantasy thoughts
Keeping in mind his power
Constantly got to know
That trouble infatuates his actions
My angelic lady you are
The only companion that I crave
I can't stop pleading your love
To erase my doubts about you
Tears of love
Without passion, without a helping hand
Realize that you are the one I need
I am the one that left the heart on the street
Wandering day and night
To find the one to dry my
Tears of Love.

Hope

As miserable I am
I toast life
This life full of mystery
I am a sinner and a liar
Since the first breath
I never recognized myself as who I am
Where I am going
What I am doing
Hope
I live lost in the depths of life
I am the Saint that betrays you
When asked about my thoughts
I live elsewhere up high
Hope
See the world from the sky
Seas, trees, caves and lost souls
Full of impurity, dying
As miserable I am
No night is dark enough to hide
A light of hope
Magnificent rays of sun will shine
Through the gray clouds
Give the joy of living
That joy isn't in me right now
Waiting for that smile
To erupt in my life.

Going to War

Love you
Were the last words
Trembling weak body
The woman told the soldier
Her plaintive voice
Carried by the wind
You will not come back
Across the chilled fields
Of frozen snow
To where her soldier fought
A lament, tears of hope
Still trembling, she whispers
Love You
As she cries in the dark room
In conquest of the truth
A voice laughs
Love was about to end
Sweet memories can betray the mind
The soldier doesn't feel the pain
Too late as the enemy strikes

Suddenly from behind
It is a war to fight
Not in the field but in the dismay of the heart
Strangely he was speaking of roses
A toast to life, red wine
Other joyful moments
Promised in a future life
How many brides will live in solitude
When war takes away the future
The first night of warm embraces
Trembling I am
The soldier told the enemy
Love has died here
His voice motionless in the wind
Heard by the silent audience
That feels behind him, before him
Going to war.

We: John, Carol and Lauren

So let me address the situation John said
Carol and Lauren listen peacefully
Sitting next to the one they love
What happened was not my intention
The plane crash was written in advance
Destiny will always take its course
God had a place for us in Heaven
To watch others and their behavior
For the past few days
We have been watching you all
We are overwhelmed to notice
The love, the passion, the tears
We are really concerned and sorry
To have created this immense turmoil
We love you all
Even before our departure
To create distress was not our intention
To you all we want to tell
Don't drown your love with tears
We are not too far from you all
Look at the sea to touch our souls
We
Are three Angels arising from the water
Sure enough to reach the sky
Because from high
We can look at you all
Hugs and a big smile
Your turn for departure will come
Days and years passing fast
You know that we are here
Waiting to be together for eternity.

Ready to Die

Many years have been going by
I can tell by the pictures
Adorning my walls
The one that speaks loud
Is my mother holding me tight
Sitting on the old rocking chair
With a faded smile
Others picture hang on the wall
That tell the story of my life.
Brothers, sisters, and friends
That have long passed.
Memories of joyful times
Ready to Die
With no regrets in life
My turn has come
I will be calm, shut my eyes
Hear voices around
Surrender to the veil of the last sky
Perhaps a kiss a gentle touch
Over the now spent body
I slowly release the doleful look
At whom I loved and gave my heart
Have the courage and the strength
To forget the remaining pain
Ready to Die
Silence, dark shadow
Going to sleep with a smile.

Revenge

Blood in your eyes
Rages to see me die
Don't tear your soul apart
I am still alive
Blood in your eyes
Would see revenge
On the world that isn't mine
Your dress of hate
Seen on your body
That revenge will make you die
Your infested soul
Will eventually burn in hell
Not even Satan will be overwhelmed
Don't cry for the sins
You have committed
Forgiveness is out the question
The only revenge is
To burn to hell
In the deep fire
Your flesh will sting
This is the way
You pay for your sins.

The Beggar

I was walking through the main road
It was snowing, and very cold
In Greenwich Connecticut my residential city
Where rich people live in absolute peace
At the corner of the road I see a beggar
Extending his trembling hand at those passing by
Eyes of innocence and an unhappy smile
It was a kid, anyone can tell
By looking at his face covered with tears
I stop for a while, wondering why.
The wet snow penetrating my body
Watching many rich people pass by
And not see one of them at least
Dignify the beggar with a smile
I got close to that kid
My hand shaking from the cold
Stopping trying for my wallet
I knew what I had was just my last dollar
Isn't much I told the kid
At least you can buy a cup of warm soup
He took that dollar without saying thanks
I knew in my heart he was overwhelmed
I keep walking to reach my destination
Still looking back at the poor kid

Sitting on the sidewalk soaking wet
Snow and tears mixing on my cheeks
I Pray and ask God why
If this is life please let me die
America. America I repeat, talking to myself
No one should beg in a country like this
I am not rich
But I got feelings for that kid
The snow coming down in a heavy manner
I thought to myself what I should do to help
Not much I said with regret
My destination I reach it was warm and safe place
I thought about that kid before I went to sleep
The morning after, the news man talking
About the beggar found frozen, dead
My guilty conscience deep in my heart
I knew I acted selfishly start to have flashbacks
Suddenly the beggar appeared next to me
With rosy cheeks and a big smile
I knew right then that he was happy in paradise
Few words he spoke before vanishing from my thoughts
"Thank you my big brother, see you when you die".

Into Eternity

Freeing you isn't my intent
In this world full of sinners
Maybe tomorrow with an insensitive heart
I will change my will
And see you flying into polluted air
In fields covered in black polluted snow
Before you get out of reach
Embrace your thoughts feeling your soul
Into Eternity
Freeing your heart
Isn't pretending falling behind
Being close to light up my life
I would like for you to stay
Cleanse the polluted air
Plant new seeds in life
No sins to hide under the sky
Departing isn't smiling it seems
Dark days with sad sun
Cold nights with hidden moon
Wrinkled sheets in a bed full of tears
Let me awake from this sad dream
If departing is your intent
Let my soul be in your company
In the exit from life.

Just Thinking

I was looking through my old written poems
Yellow are the pages from time past
Abandoned in a ripped shoebox
I want to search for the one to send to you
Hours went by to find the right one
Tired and disappointed I said to myself
Stop this nonsense and write a new one
Good or bad whether brings smile or tears to you
For all the emotions that daily we go through
Just few new words to write
Thinking of you
I can surely relate to your inside feelings
For I too am imprisoned in your soul
When I react to the external approach of life
Instead listen to the emotional inside
What I chose to say related to you
I can take control to create something new
It isn't too late to start living in reality
Responsibility for the life to be
I truly mean what I write
No matter if it makes sense or not
With God's guidance we can reach the sky
Touch unlimited universal sites

Just Thinking

You should be the one that guides
To the right path of life
Never forget that God is on your side
He will give you the strength you need
For a better future
I said enough for now
You'll know what I've written in time
Just read the new ones
That remind you about what I said in the past
Life with you always will be.
And never forget it's everlasting.

Leave God Alone

Leave God alone
Senseless human being
Worm of the earth
Taking advantage of your supreme post
You that sit on the high chair
Above all living creations
How you can judge
If you are blinded by your own actions
The stable you reside in is a castle because your power
Isn't the creation of the Holy One.
Justice isn't for all you imply from the high
I am the God here on earth
Crawl under me
My words are the law for you
Leave God Alone
I implore with tears in my eyes
God's laws were written centuries before
You were sitting high
Let me reply
Honorable supreme dressed in power
The air that you breathe can't be purified
Because your actions are scum
That is the reason you got hired
The day will come for you to step down
From the high chair you sit on now
That day we all will be equal
No one standing aside and being divided
So you
My honorable and supreme brother
Be alert to your how actions
Never mention in vane God's name
Just step down and think of your past.

Lost Behind a Dream

Something strange inside me
Erodes my soul, I can't feel my body
I am numb, can't sleep
The pillow is my companion
I find myself looking through the dark window
Of nights past
Waiting to see the new day born
I feel I am dying
I got to erase thoughts of sadness
Give my soul hope of happiness
Can't live the rest of my life
Looking through the window
On the world outside
Be a shadow
Tears filling my eyes
Thinking of the past life
Lived with sincere happiness
That gives joy and sadness
I want to live
Asking myself why the door is shut
I got no answers
Continue dreaming
Waiting for that day to come
That will give me the strength
To open that door
And discover that happiness
Could be reality

Never Make It

The word around the town was
Never going to make it
In this part of the country
Where expectations are too high
I thought they were right
My hopes started to die
He is never going to make it
Families said at night around the table
We pray he might
I sense to quit
When the problems arise
I got to make an effort
Just to try
So I clear up my thoughts
Something in my spirit lagged
Got to act quickly, stop dragging
I got to make it
No excuse to find
In this part of the country
Where expectations are high
I manage any way I could
To make it day by day
The secret was just say a prayer
No doubt about it
I did, I made it
And I'm going to stay.

Awake Me

Awake me in the morning

Let's enjoy one more day

Too many matters to accomplish

Many favors to thank

The kid in school I got to rush

Going to the office I got to work

Awake me in the morning

Let me see the new horizon

Of a born day

Let me see the sun

Walk from the sky to the sea

Breathing the fresh air

Making the day fly away

My matters all completed

Let me thank the Lord

To give me a hand

To live one more day

Time is going, my departure is near

Awake me in the morning

If my heart still responds

Let me step on the green grass

Enjoying the memory

Of my life past.

Me and the World

I was born in a stable
Sleeping with horses and sheep
What did I do to this world
To deserve such a treat
Never ask for anything more
Before my life was long gone
I died as soon I was born
In this desolate world
Waiting for God to be my savior
To clean the polluted soil of this world
Politicians saturated in sins
In the stable can't see a thing
Just rumors of horses and sheep
To keep me warm when I go to sleep
To this world I don't say thanks
Giving me a life and more surprises
The stable is my home that keeps me alive
Gives me a space from the population
Me and the world are separated
I don't want to live with sins
When death will knock at the door
No one alive will know
I was the one that lived alone
Born and died in the stable
Never ask for anything more.

Reservations in this World

Reservations I have
To meet this new generation
Of human beings
Specialize in dismantling the entire universe
I that never see a spent star fall and die
From the high of the mountains
Why have I been chosen to
Encounter this unholy event
What I have done so wrong
To deserve this cruel task
I that believe in the Holy word
Called binding
Giving me the tender love to embrace
Not a body joy to erase
World Oh world I scream
I am so sad
Why torment me with this task
Why punish me from the beginning
To meet this new generation
Of human beings
Reservations I have
I will deny this matter
Run where I can't hide
From the destruction of the creation
Waves of mutilation resist the temptation
Of the world's resolution.

Wondering

I walk alone in this great State
From the flat lands to the mountains
Rocks and trees are the main attraction
To be where I am
Got to be brain washed
The woods are a city that never sleeps
Where life is alive and well kept
Wondering
Wasn't my intention to move here
Along the road a light I see
Oh Lord I cry
Give me a helping hand
To find my way around
And reach the town
Venture in dark blessings
All the Saints keep me company
Guide me on the right path
Has been months and years
That I have been wondering
Do I belong here
Where progress has stopped
The light gone far
Can't be reached
I got to find my way back
Into the city of sinners

Going over the Line

Give me some space I got to move on
Can't stay here and decay my soul
Inch by inch I will crawl into the dust
To reach the boundary of my salvation
Going over the line
I have been down for so long
I need a fresh air to breathe
Before I suffocate
I got to move fast before it is too late
My life runs short and that's my fate
Please get me there don't stop now
I need some help to cross the finish line
My dream is vanished if I stay here
I feel in my bones that death is near
Going over the line
Maybe I will reach
What I was looking for
A wishful site of an open door
A dark light that I never saw before
Showing the way I got to hold on
Now I am on the other side of my future
I can see clear I can breathe
I went over the line
Where dreams came true
Just smiling at life, nothing more.

Today's World

Who's this guy that attempts to control the world
Bringing up lies of days ahead
Killing the hopes that everyone dreams
Today's World
From East to West
From the North to the South
We creatures get burned
We got to take turns
He may be the devil in a human spirit
Killing everything around in his sight
Today's World
We are tired to live
You suffocate us
You are the crazy guy giving me death
You tore down my dreams of success
Since no one knows how you got elected
You have chained us
With any sacred question
Who are you that makes laws
Without any cause
In time you will answer
All the aggravating questions
Not to us creatures
But to the One living above

My Child

Tonight you act so strangely
Your docile voice is trembling
Tell me love what's on your mind
I will be man enough
Think and take my time
Talk to me my lovely creature
Whatever it is I am here to listen
Trembling body tears in her eye
She tells me the truth can't be hidden
Remember she said
When we were together
All night long embracing
We said forever
Time now has come
That the seed has germinated
I carry your child in my womb
For an instant I fell into sincere thoughts
Then tears in my eyes start to shine
Don't worry I said
Give her a kiss and a smile
For the fault of love you give me a child
I will be responsible it's my intention
Be with you two
Will be time well spent
You the mother of my child
Whoever thought
That one night of games
Would have changed my life.

Waiting

We spend our time here waiting
Time never realized
All the questions in mind
We fight, laugh at the sight
Sure we need an answer that is right
Waiting
Life is an adventure
A journey into our minds
Till we find the reason
To stop dying
Nothing is enough to anticipate
The moment has ended
Time is over I tell you my friends
You too my brothers and sisters
Don't cry into this wall of pain
Keep your broken heart well sound
Waiting
Search the other side
Don't give up now find the time
Maybe a pure companion
That vanishes in the sky
Where her soul from the high
Let's you know that you need time
Don't give up now
Time has come for us to smile
The waiting is over
Whatever I was looking for, I find it
The one that will guide me
To the end of time

The Call

The phone rings
One time, ten times
Twelve o'clock at night
The stars illuminating the sky
She isn't
It would have been nice if she was here
Who cares I will go away
With my thoughts our souls are lost
The world is mine
I walk on water in the pond
The moon on my side
My image reflected above in the sky
I am a man or not
My freedom is gone
Night of love I should have had
Lonely, she knows I am dying
I don't look back
She's away I deserve that
Fighting in the streets
With who I don't know
I don't want to know
Repented
I am a man or not
It's normal what I said
Special days are gone, good bye
We will be rivals
The world is mine
Clouds I will see in the sky
The nights are quiet for now
Out is her word around
Oh God savior
Give me a good night

What I can Say

What I can say about you
That you want me to say
Silence is the answer
You only know what I want to say
I want you to know
I will wait to say it
What I can say
I will wait when you are grown
I will wait when you are awake
Close your eyes for an instant
Stop searching for an answer
In the season when flowers blossom
You are the first creature of dreams
Smiling but your vision is a ghost
What I can do still waiting
What I can say about him
He knew it
Maybe he does know it
He does not speak
Just listen in silence stop for a moment
No smile in the garden of Eden
For you to satisfy yourself
Stop chatting, committing sins
Isn't an answer
What I can say
You are the one to realize what you did wrong
For us the way it was
A dream of the past
What I can say about you
I don't want to say it

Dark Room

Kids in the street playing
Dark is the day never get tired
Selling love is the secret
Mothers and fathers between them
Believe the faces of innocent
Kids on the streets
Giving to the world
The silent love
Mothers and daughters
Plying, selling love into the spent sun
Stay for few more minutes
Say more to this world closed in a
Dark room
As the secret of you lives with pride
For the love that you give
You crying eyes telling lies
You all know where love is
The beauty tells the world about it
Selling love isn't the answer
Soon or later we got to find a solution
A man and a woman are nothing
Alone they got to win
Do not vanish into the spent sun
Dark Room
Kids in the street no more
Time has expired walk with me
Into the pride of true love
Isn't a sin now
Your eyes can't lie
You're the one who knows why.

Ghosts at the Beardsley Park

I was in heaven at Beardsley park
Once a garden, now a crypt
Two shadows hide, two ghost figures
Pale lips, eyes shut, dead faces
Not long ago
Flowers and trees were companions
Of the loved one
We too enjoyed the site and perfume
Of the green grass
A kiss, a smile, a few words about the future
Countless hours, time of happiness
We cherished that place
We took an oath for life
Two untiring eternal lovers
Now two shadows haunt this cheerless place
The scent, the smiles vanish
Flowers and trees dried
Tears of sorrow all over the Park
Those days of lies are gone
What we shared
Wonderful memories
Were the steps taken
By two ghosts
At the Beardsley Park.

The Stranger

The party started in a boisterous mood
She quietly got close and murmured
Can't stay here I am going crazy
Let's go into my room it's quiet and peaceful
No one will know what we do and what we don't
I am the stranger
Invited to the party, got to think
Quickly before it gets too wild
Still shocked for the outcome
I don't know if it's real or it's a dream
Inside her room there is no tension
I wasn't feeling like a stranger
She hugged me and said relax
I do what I want this is my house
Slowly, slowly love happened
I was shocked but not surprised
We don't say a word for few moments
Someone was breathing inside the room
With a caress she said stay cool
A figure appeared in front of us
She looked at me and started to laugh
A crying voice I heard said
Why do you do this I don't deserve it
I was the stranger inside the room
She was telling him: You are still the one
They embraced and wept
For how long, who knows
My time had come to leave the scene
Slowly, and quietly I opened the door
That was the end of my part of the story
I never turned back to see where I stood
I knew for both of them I was a stranger.

Littleton (New Hampshire)

Here in Littleton, where the wind scrapes the side of the mountain
Swinging from the old oak tree are his leaves making a majestic sound
The days and years are like the jet stream of an eagle speeding to site for prey
Shrubs on side roads are nests for cicadas and owls
Giving them time to search when night approaches.
Green meadows drawing straight horizons
Splendor of stars in the month of March
A hundred forests embellish the sites.
The smell of pine cones, songs of birds giving tranquility to my soul
Many dreams of journeying to a chaotic city where I came from
Tears of repentance days of joy clouds of people on the streets
Cars polluting the air so used like daily bread
Littleton; white is your color, pure is the air where gentleness is a must
Tears of sorrow disappear. With the risen sun life starts
Thoughts of joy for coming days, singing about the wind and trees
Mountains, snow and serenity of living in this paradise
You our God give us the gift to ponder in silence our repentant thoughts
You our God who gave us your servant, the teachings from the top of the hill
Where your house stands
We praise His words which keep us united in this paradise we call. Littleton.

Son of the Past Love

A gentle touch at your breast
Feeling your heart beat fast
The blood running like a river
Two shadows standing in the silent room
Thinking of the son of the past love
Dark is the sky
No moon to light up our fragile life
I am not there my shadow died
Fun and love are memories of the past
When just a touch
Would have sparked love to last
You still in the dark room
Standing with sober eyes
Waiting to get tired
Feeling my shadow
Son of the past love
You've got more to come
The night is still young
For you to die
Give me a reason to be here
For you to spark my soul
Let me come alive.

Good Morning to All

Awaken by the rays of the sun
Filtering from the curtains of my room
Open my eyes. I said:
Good morning life
Good morning sun
Thanks to you God to give me another day
Good morning breeze for the pure fresh air
Good morning grass blades
Waving with shiny dew
That perfume, the meadow around
Good morning singing birds
To keep me company with gentle song
Good morning flowers
With the radiant colors give me a smile
Good morning to you all
My soul is dancing
I am happy and free
Embrace this life for what it is giving me
Thank you I said to you all
Hoping tomorrow will be
A beauty you reserve for me.

Searching

Behind the tree of thoughts
Into the valley of reflection
I am waiting to fly into the sky
Amid of spirit feel my body high
Where I may find myself
Through a garden into the clouds
Alone no flames to be my guide
The wind blowing gentle
Carrying through my mind
Sitting in the cloud
An Angel said Hi
With a loud voice I reply
I am searching to reach the high sky
He smiled.
Keep flying he said
You got a ways to go yet
Don't look back
The finish line you will see
When you stop searching for He.

You Are

You are wiser that you know
Wonder of wonders
How this can be more courageous
Without fear you live
You are stronger than you feel
Seeking whatever you desire
The greatness of your soul
And the quality to be admired
You younger than years tell
Never revealing the truth to be
You can hold joy and tears
And everything else
You are meant to be
So special beyond your dreams
Divine is your life more than you think
Accept what you've got
A gift, your mind
Is a miracle wonderful to share.

Her Memory

From an empty bed
Sheets wet from tears
Of melancholy thoughts
The memory of her living
Gives me the strength
To enlighten the gloomy room
From her beautiful lips
Her gilded smile reminds of time past
Her sweet body, the velvet skin
Her green eyes repose
Glimpse at the naked body
Omnipotent of the firmament
That gives me life
Don't let the thoughts of her die
Gather our hearts in one
Her Memory
Would have make me happy
Where are you that you vanished
Roaming from heart to heart
I have nostalgia of your vanished kisses
My nights are far from over
I hold you in my thoughts
Sweet body in the empty bed
I will never forget.

That Name

I scream in this wretched night
Why suffer before I die
Alone in the room no place to hide
I call that name
Don't ask me why
That name dies between my lips
That name that is hard to pronounce
My heart my soul they cry
That name inside me I have
My body is drained
From the continuous scream
I am tired. Dark all over
The immense sadness crushes my spirit
My lips dry, arid, hurting
For the continuing call
My tongue is frozen
Nothing exists anymore
I feel the suffering
The pain explodes
That name
My life expires.

How Lucky I Am

If I would have met you before
I would not have acted like a little child
It is you that wakes me in the morning
And cover me at night before falling asleep
I want anyone to know
That I will do anything for you
I will wander all over the city
Without a destination
I will die if this is my destiny
For her green eyes I will live
Another life
It would be beautiful if we find each other
Ride the merry go round with the horses
Fight the sun
To look into each other eyes
The melodic music from the horses' mouth
Suggest a harmonic singing
How lucky I am
The life that I have is just for her
I am happy I am joyous
Because we found each other
She said:
You are a man of value
Never give up fight with your heart
I know you will prevail
Fight to the end
I believe in her
Because of her I will fight to the end.

Dreams are Real

Awaken in a sweetest vision

With sunshine bathing your pretty body

No walls can stop the rays

Penetrating the room of sins

Dreams are real

You next to me in the deepest passion

Wet from unstopping motion

Chilling trembling turning

Now that my gentle touch merges to you

Making its way deep into your heart

Isn't a dream, this is real

The lovely harmony flows into your soul

It's strange that this ardent love is mine

The end is near I feel the shock

Getting back from the journey

The sins finally ending

My thoughts are yours now

How to build a castle of real dreams

Feeling the blond hair looking through your eyes

Lighting up the coldest night

This dream is real

You are here to stay, you are mine

We rule together our love

The time will wrinkle bodies

Drying up the sweat odors

Once a start of surrounding motions

Now flowers will blind our life

Sending out fragrant aroma

That reminds us of our body's sweat.

You Talking

I hear the words that you spoke
Time has passed, I am still crying
My last drop of tears
Running deep into my skin
I see your shadow face
You Talking
My heart is broken
My life restrained in these gloomy walls
I wish I can turn around
See some light reality not a mirage
Your eyes are full of fear
I don't know what to do
Thinking every day and praying
I hope that will come the day
That I awake up seeing the green eyes
No fear but just smiles
Listen to you talking
About our lives.

Calling

I don't understand
I am confused
I make a call
My lips don't move
If the world knew what I feel
For sure we can start a conversation
I am such a fool
To be lonely
That's the reason I call
I would make changes if I could
I would ask this heart of mine
To give the universe my love
Time will end my suffering
I am on fire
Someone please answer my call
Listen to my confusing thoughts
Help me if anyone can help
Don't let me die.

Blind Vision

What Blind vision I had
Unreasonable thinking about the surroundings
My white race was supreme
No wrong answer
What choice I had
Blind Vision of selfishness
Give me help if you can
You will not regret
Let me see over the line
Of white supremacy
For my sins let me pay my debt to society
Stop the tears falling from my eyes
I want to enjoy the sparkling sky
I would give faith to the world
No more shaking ground
Brotherhood in the darkness of the night
The war is over forget the past
Faith in the world
Be honest about it, forget my faults
Blind Vision no more

The Man on the Hill

I am not from this country
I hope you can tell
People around ask me that question
Since I made the move
From the cemented city
To the forested mountains of New Hampshire
When I speak my accent is supreme
Hope they understand.
The man on the hill
They call me
In the morning I scream
Hey Americans with open arms
From the first day that I came
You gave me shelter and new life
Every day full of surprises
Day by day time went by
New ideas always in mind
I will repay you all
For letting me stay
This what I said forty years later
The man on the hill
I will be remembered
When the morning turns to night
And no scream is heard from the mount.

My Son One Day

It's been a year or more
Since I've seen my son
He was waiting for me
Embarrassed I can tell
Today he said
I would like to talk to you
I didn't ask him why
I am here to listen I said
You've got my blood flowing in your veins
I see tears coming down
Trembling sounds from his lips arise
You know the bridge of silence
It isn't because love for you fell
I just want to be like you if I can
It was wrong I am at fault
It took some time to understand
My door is open for you
The past has vanished from my thoughts
You're my father he said I am happy
To be that way
My son one day appeared
That smiling face pure
My turn has come to say the words
I too was untruthful about what happened
I have my faults and that is a fact
I learned with time about life
That the world isn't selfishness
Reality gets to the finish line
Where the son and the father
Are united to the end of time

Thoughtful

One night of bitter agony

I lay in bed and started to cry

I was scared of the dark outside

To take a walk don't think about it

Everything was taken

From my manhood

Now I am standing alone

I've got to choose find a solution

Talk to the Lord for help

And find an answer

Given a set of circumstances

I started to talk in dimensional thoughts

The task wasn't easy

To be one of the happy people

Start enjoying life and laugh about it

Immortal I am laughing and crying

When happiness arise someday smiling

Slowly my agony turns to love

The prayer was answered stopping the turmoil

No more bitterness

The dark turned to light

I get up from the bed

Running and reaching a new life.

To my Mother's Memories

The departure of that smile
That keeps my life alive
Makes my days sad and gray
No more days of reunion to chat
But solitary thinking about the past
My mother isn't here anymore
She's going to a place full of darkness
Where the sun will never be warm
Where the sound of the sons' voices
Can never be heard in that far way place
February 26 will be the anniversary
Of sadness for years to come.

Women Coming and Going

Women coming and going
From my bed at night
Having wings at their feet
To fly over for love
Women with no sense of life
Just thinking about money
And selling what they have
Bodies with no heart
Women coming and going
From bed at night
They got the key in their hands
These bodies with no heart
Long and beautiful naked legs
Ready to send signals for sins
Pistol in one hand
Close to your brain
Do not forget to pay when all ends
Women to be watched
Staying in bed night and day
Fake rumors and orgasm
Women coming and going.

No Sense Talking

I heard a rumor on the street
That you will leave for new adventures
Crossing the mountains to reach the sea
Just to get away from me
I got to think how to solve
And stop this no sense talking
Your heart for sure is broken
The lies causing the damage
Isn't true what they said
The flame inside is there
It wasn't just a bet that I made
To get into you and then forget
I have a heart too that causes pain
If the bit isn't the same will die
No sense talking
Will stop the flow of blood
Will stop the fire below their eyes
The crying and salty tears
Never to be tasted on your dry skin
If you go life will go on
No sense talking all over town
My name will fly
For the devotion that I have
Don't go I said
Your adventure will start here again
Blue sky and shining star at night
You name written all over town
No more. No sense talking
Will make you cross the mountain.

My Star is Here

I encounter moments of joy in my life
Since I was born to now
Love was on my side
Family and friends always smile
This was the way my day went by
Time came when I said good bye
To family and friends and even some smiles
My star is here
In this country that I embrace
That gave me new life and much more appreciation
Work was a must
Love came second to all
The song I learned that speaks about love
It made me aware in life we've got to share
My star is here
I will never depart I got nothing more
In this life to ask
My world now so different
Even if smiles are hard to come by
At night I stand alone watching the sky
Always waiting for that star
That gives me the shine on my life.

Midnight in the Woods of New Hampshire

The sound of the grandfather clock on the wall
Tells me that midnight has just come
I am sitting on the rocking chair in front my wood burning stove
The flame of burning wood is gone
But the metal still hot keeps me warm.
It is silent into the wooden house where I live
Midnight in the woods of New Hampshire
Are beautiful and loud
The moon illuminates my lawn and trees around
The stars dancing at the sounds of the infinite universe
I would like to go out and admire
But looking through the window I realize
That this is the time for the wildlife to be out
The loud noise that I hear from inside my house
Is a talk between them hard to understand
They all speak different languages
Who is barking, howling, singing
It is a concert of beautiful hymns
I get a chair sit close to the window
Tired I am but I want to enjoy the free concert that I hear

See the main attraction of the recital
Raccoons picking through a feast of roots of dead trees
Can hear their teeth digging deep
The deer chewing on leaves of the green trees
Moose, wolves, animals of all species
And sometimes even a bear
It is a show that can't be missed.
Pine needles flying all over the lawn
The early morning wind clears the way
For a sunny day to come
No sleep yet still the sounds of the birds
Keeps me awake after the wild ones are gone
Scattered in the green sanctuary of the woods
Midnight in the woods of New Hampshire
Wasn't a dream, I got to stop smiling at the scene
For tonight the show is over
My eye lids close it is time to said good bye
Go to sleep and be ready for another night.

Nothing Left

What have you got left in your soul
That wasn't mine
I was the perpetrator that went inside
I broke all the rules that you had
Nothing is intact in your body
Hours and days we got lost in love making
Tireless not shame and sweat of joy
Time has cancelled the loving approach of life
Don't worry you will have someone come around
I know what life is all about
This someone else will come for the ride
Because you got nothing left inside
Your blond hair faded now
Your green eye losing their sight
You lips lost the smile and went dry
Everything you got left is fake now
Nothing left
The word spread
Don't try to change or maybe to hide
One thing I suggest and it isn't right
Just think of the fun you had
When your body had everything inside.

Divine Love

In and out through my whole being
Perfect in every part of my soul
I thank God for His divine love
The work He's done is not governed
But the outer cycle
Went around and has risen
I have fallen through the years of turning
Asking for a hand nothing in return
In the years of my life
Divine Love was most
Freedom and joy turn to love
Hibernate to slow me down
Always return to start on time
Is God's renewal that greatly bless
To raise me from the fall
Divine Love
Makes new again
My heart
Don't stay in line waiting for your turn
Just jump in front
To share the Divine Love.

Contemporary

Walking down the main drag
Stop at the corner and get my thoughts
Want to light a cigarette
Looking cool for the passers by
Hat and sunglasses
Unbuttoned shirt showing my chest hair
Hoping to attract at least one smile
Time has changed my look has faded
This is not the new contemporary.
Few more minutes I said, let me stay
To see the changes that time has made
I had no time to reflect on my thoughts
When few teenagers passing close
And give me the look
Turning my head the only thing I saw
The kids underwear the pants below the knees
Hey man one of them screaming
This what you see we call
Contemporary
Maybe you don't understand
The kids are together
That look that you have is not contemporary
Contemporary I reply
Looking at myself in the store window
Time has changed my looks died.

The Fallen Oak

I remember that tree so big
Branch large arms to shadow the complete yard
In the hot days of summer
When the sun was a king
And rays of fire dried the ground
No refuge for us Kids
Running for the oak tree
Protector it has been for generations past
My mother and father used it as refuge
That's what they said, I wasn't there yet
Now the fallen oak lies dead
No more extended arms
To welcome the sweating gently
Give rest on the hot day
People walking by stop
The fallen oak smiles in remembrance
And sins committed on that shadow
The leaves are dry lie on the ground
They too are dead
Showing the unrest
No more singing from a mother bird
With food on her beak
The young scream to eat
I stand under the sun no more shadow
Seeing the fallen oak getting old and dry
Few days have passed the fallen oak vanished
Chain saw and logger clean the site
Where a lonely nightingale searches
For a nest that isn't there.

Show in the Street

Run, run a loud voice
Interrupts the usual walk of thousands
Of people on the way to life
What happened the old lady asks
Talking to no one.
A mother dressed in black kneels
Tears and blood mixed on the ground
Help her soft voice whispering to the air
Fake looks of people never seen before
Murmuring words from dry lips
Tragedy has struck again
Show in the street
Is it reality or just a scene
No one seeing what happened
It is the name of the game
Few strange tears wet the ground
It is a free sad show.
No actress no applause from the spectators
The scene change when a coffin appears
To understand the play to see and believe
Show in the street
Five hours of standing no more tears
No murmuring words fill the air
The tragedy is over life goes on
Start to walk again to a destination unknown
Waiting for a new script
And for tomorrow to come

My House

Walking inside my trailer house

The walls are straightened from the bottom up

Water all around making my feet soaked

Tennis shoes no socks all wet

The walls made of carbon box

Painted for look of a white stain

My house is a castle

And I am the king of all the surroundings

Frigid nights coming

Covered the icy corners with newspaper

Street lights illuminating my room

The gilded approach to a miserable life

No guests are coming making me excited

I do pray at night for the sun to come out

For my walls to dry in my house

A solution I need before another frigid season comes

Can't wait any longer to destroy the carbon box.

Ideas

Let's be honest my friends
Don't just talk without making any sense
We know that we are wrong
Don't look outside from the inside
Take a chance go take a walk
See if your feet will take you
In the right direction
Ideas we have to make better
We are mortals, maybe we are not
We are not angels to fly away
Hide ourselves behind the clouds
Maybe the ideas are just words
To find the reason not to die
Day after day alone in my thoughts
Talking about a better way
Maybe love is the answer
Waiting for another day
Sooner or later the sun has to shine again
If the rain comes down
It will draw my thoughts
Hope to not be alone
And talk about new ideas
Love comes first
We know that hurt is normal
At the end we stop, that was stupid
Let's go far away
The intentions are there.

Here to Stay

The world revolves around the axle
The force of nature shows that
Whatever goes up must come down
To many of us,
Scary thoughts when we look at the sky
I would run if I can find a place to hide.
Here to stay
Let's try to not think about
That life is a cycle that eventually fades away
Tell me your thoughts, say something
Even a lie I accept
Open your mouth let me smell your breath
I will see the truth if it is there
Here to Stay
I get confused when reality shows her face
Too late to recap the events
We are here together to find a solution
Deep into the night I will not sleep
I walk slowly in the dark room
A candle lightens the corner desk
I write my feelings from the events
Trying to put some magic in past times
Some days just irony to be alone
The destiny is written in a ghost town
The breathing is easy when death is near
Can't run away
Tears coming down, no solution is there
Sadness will take over the smiling thoughts
Reality will keep you company
Before the sunrise will lighten the sky
Illuminating the dark chamber
Where we will all be for eternity.

Leave me Alone

Don't rise me from my death bed
Don't take me out of my refuge
I don't want to smell this stinking society
I will not live this nonsense life
Leave me Alone
The scenery is the same
I don't want to hear
I don't want to see the one alive
My departure from society is permanent
Let me enjoy the quietness
My perpetual rest
Where no laws change the daily basis
The commander is out there
Ruling how to breathe
To survive you got to obey
Leave me Alone
I want to remain here
In the darkness of this in cave space
No voices of lamenting people
No tears to wet the ground
No black veil covering the faces
No smiling approach to life
Why go out to see what is real.
Leave me alone.

Orphan Baby Boy

Walking into the muddy war camp
A crying voice alerts me I am not alone
Dead bodies, ammunitions and guns
Scattered all over the scary site
The laments I follow
Baby boy in the mud
Left alone in the middle of the road
His mother corpse lies next to him
The father gone for sure into the war
Why memories of joy
Turn sad that site
War and destruction made the boy cry
I look at him drying his eyes
Reading his thoughts and ask why
I stand next to him for awhile
Giving some comfort then say good bye.
Orphan baby boy eventually will die
I had no choice in this matter
Why they let him be born in this cold war
Then leave him orphan
In the mud at the crossroads.

Leaving Earth

Life has given me everything
Time has come for my departure
Nothing will pleasure my stay
Doesn't make any sense
For me to be here
Leaving Earth
What I saw I can't deny
I stay still, I don't think about it
My dry skin goes down the hill
I've been giving my soul to earth
I should never give up trying
Because the soil is mine
The sweat from my body
Flowing down the river
The sweet water is salty now
Creating a pool of joyful play
Leaving Earth
Thinking about the sins committed
That for sure they will drag me down to hell
Few days are left to look around
Maybe repair the damage that I've done
Hiding I cried out and said sorry
To any one I hurt here in this earth
Give me the strength to open my lips
Let me give all a smile and find a guide
Above is my final destination
The Supreme waiting His arms open
Leaving Earth
Maybe I will find what I search for
No more sins and sweaty encounters
Looking down from the high clouds
I send a message to the humans below
Think before you sin, look above
My shadow will tell the pain to pay.

I Am

Unpredictable I have been told I am
The craziness showing in my actions
Selfishness and sorrow make me who I am
Sometimes bashful will be the reason why
I Am
In captivity of the universe
Who is in charge commands making new rules
Female or male that sits on the high chair
Persecuting me
Seducing me
Charming me before the final act of killing
Affectionate is the look given
Promised to my heart that into eternity
I will carry and follow their laws
I Am
The one who stands in the middle of the night
Counting the hours to the next day when light will come
The officers are here in my pathway
To direct my soul into another world
In captivity I will be for the rest of my life
I will be unpredictable so take me
Do whatever is written
I can't stay here I am not welcome
My days of standing are over.

Missing Time

It's been a long time now
That my room has the shades down
No artificial light works to illuminate
This empty room, it is sad and dark
The sun is a strange something is missing
Her eyes where the light
Giving bright vision
It is her that is missing
It is her that runs away from my vision
I need light, I need to see where I am going
The clock in the square day after day
Makes the same sound
Time passing by, silver hair showing age
Can't wait any longer, she's got to come back
I want to feel that she is near
Smelling her scent
Missing Time
Has been the main reason
Her vision can bring back the brightness
Lighting the empty room
The emptiness is bigger than the sea
It is her that is missing, she flew away
The clock still makes the same sound
I will never lose hope
I feel she is near, I feel she is back
Her eyes illuminating that empty room
The sun's rays infiltrate the downed shades
Warm sensations through my body
Tells me that it is time for love.

Nature

Under a cherry tree I sit
Reflecting on my thoughts
The singing birds keep me company
Enjoying the fruitful branch
I hear the brook singing
The sound of the limpid water stumbles
Over the rolling stones
Listening and watching nature
Taking her course
A concert of unusual sounds
Tells me about creatures around
Lifting my vision over the mountains
Where the peaks are covered in a white mantle
In the green valley
The heard grace in a peaceful mood
The tired sun requests a rest
From a sweating working day
Still looking at nature
The almost dark and transparent sky
Sending out the stars and the moon to scrutinize
As the deep night infiltrates
The painted picture of the immortals rest.

Fall is Here

The warm and sunny days are going
The long days of light are memories of the past
From my shut window
I enjoy the changing of the leaves
From the sparkling green
To brown drying already dying
Fall is here
The blowing wind playing with the tired trees
Old branches falling down
From hard work of the summer past
The leaves on the pathway protect the green grass
The spend sunny rays going to sleep
Behind the grey clouds
Playing games with the immortal creature
Fall is here
The mad clouds
Unleash the rage of a violent thunderstorm
No singing birds adorning the sky
Only the smell of asphalt left behind
It's time now to sit down
Reflecting on the time past by
Looking at the rain coming down
Smiling at the thoughts of a new
Season yet to come.

The News

Wait!!! Wait.
This is the only word
That everybody spoke for awhile
Remember these days
Not one of us can be alone
The news was the main attraction
Telling everyone what had happened
Broken promises for better future
When challenge was on the corner
Televisions all blast we knew that guy
He was a gentleman
He didn't breathe he died
How did this happen I ask myself
We talk about life because we had faith
Remember the basic the future is safe
No one's got to die we all will prevail
The news still on
Wait!!! Wait
The reporter announces
On the screen he laughs
He doesn't know what to say.

One Night Stand

Wake up beautiful lady
The night is over
It is time you get dressed
Wake up beautiful lady
The party is over
Go back where your life shines
Today is a new day
You got to show the new face
I got to let you go
Green eyes with bitter heart
You got to go and show
That million dollar smile
To another guy.
Watch out beautiful lady
They wait for you out there
I am the one that gave you a night
You won't find a gentleman like me
That saves your soul
After a night of smiles
Wake up beautiful lady
I got to step out, I am ready
I got to run
My place is out there
Where you ladies wait
For one night stand.

Today's Young Generation

Young generation on the lookout
For ladies with no age
Young generation available
For ladies to give what they want
Young generation with long hair
Sitting at the bar waiting
No smoking ladies like fresh breath
Young generation says yes
To the ladies with no age
They pay the final tab
The car is ready just waiting
They drive to the final destination
Ferrari, Lamborghini no more limousine
This is the new living
Telling stupidly to make believe
Fake caresses of illusions
The ride is short everything is ready
Young generation have all in their hands
Few words of love
Silk sheets ready for sin
No words are spoken just soft fake touches
Clothing off muscle and wrinkle mixing
Love making with shut eyes
Noisy murmuring makes the stage
Of what young generation is today.

A Fact of Reality

I too am looking around to find out who I am
In the landscape of this Earth
I am a subject and I will be here for a while
This is the world beneath my feet
That I will be walking day after day
It's a fact established at my birth
My ancestors wrote the book
I just follow instruction and obey
The water of the sea has a reason to be
I know how many creatures are there
In the deep where my feet can't reach
Where my eyes can't see or feel with my hand
I am a subject of the wind whirling around
I look around to find a place to stand
A fact of reality
Looking at the universal sky
Sun, moon, stars, endless in their path
Scared by the suspense that has no end
There are meanings and facts to discuss
I try to explore the unfolding story
I as a subject a tiny dot
Into a scheme of mystery abound
Standing looking and flying above the clouds

A Gift for You

I never would have understood
Why I should die for her
I am in peace with my soul
Even when she is far apart from me
I miss the smell in the room
We share gestures but that is not all
I will defend myself
From the evil approaching
Hidden behind the camouflage
The faces and voices memories now
A gift for you
I hope you feel the inner meaning
Beneath the time of rejects
I will not think about the past
She was and is my woman
I will defend her with my close eyes
Suggesting a credible unity
Sharing the closeness and feelings
I will always say yes
Unfolding and revealing me to her
My heart humbly appealing
That time and age fly away with the wind
And I always will be remembered
As a man loved as a rebel
As a poet with a gift

World, New Beginning

The whole world is broken
Isn't worth it to be fixed
It's time to start all over again
Make a new beginning
There is too much suffering and pain
I love life we need a new approach
We got to wake up and look around
Assess what's going on
All the few happier endings
Give us tears and smiles
World new beginning start all over
Fragments and pieces
That once joined together part of living
Now too many stand alone
Too much separation
New beginning start all over
We got to resolve the problem
Let's break the chain of suffering
Let's break the cycle of sadness
We can learn together
Let's put in motion the use of praying
That we can change our life
For a better living
The broken world that we live
Has to be fixed now time is essential
Rebuild don't fight about how
Understand the time has come
We need to make new symbols
We need to use new languages
Redefine the world for a new beginning.

You and Me

Come here, look the way it's raining outside
If we go out now we get soaked
Let stay inside and admire
The beauty of nature
I see not far a small sun ray
Eventually this rain's got to stop
Come close who cares about
Gray skies and wet clouds
The sun isn't far, it will be born again
The twitter of a nightingale
Will tell about how blue the skies are
Caressing her hand
Excuse me do you live alone
Why that big bed
I live in a fantastic world
Give me a smile the rain almost stopped
I would have called you love
I will stay the sun will warm us
I should go, still raining very softly
We enjoy the rain from the inside
Your hand calls for love to come.

Do You Know Love

If you know what love it is
Tell me how long it has been
Since I gave you my body
How far we have traveled together
That keeps us tied for eternity
I have to follow the road that you choose
Because I feel I am part of you
Nothing will be like you
It is nothing to understand
Everything around that you build
Is just for us to be together
The ocean blue
The green leaves on the trees
Sounds of a celestial choir
The brown bricks that keep us warm
In the castle where love is
No suffering days
For the mistakes that we made
No shivering secrets for eternity
I will give share everything
Time will always keep our souls smiling
It would be not a wonderful dream
Reality will stand on infinite love.

Infinite Thinking

Don't say a word just go I will wait for you
The surrounding nature will mark your absence
They will be reborn the day of your return
I too will awake from infinite thinking
Love will fly from my heart into your cupped hand
Washing the departure face
You can if you want show to the world around you
A world that does not understand
What a faraway heart feels in the absence of care
This is why I will wait stealing imaginary touches
Infinite thinking will renew the promise we made
Time will not erase the memories in our hearts
Throughout your journey I will lead you
Accompany you in safe places
My shadow will protect your soul from sin
I still will wait here
Dreaming of your unknown whereabouts
Picturing the scene when you will return
Time to be spent in an isolated room
No more imaginary touches or imaginary kisses
I will be awake with the soft wind touching my body
It is not a dream feeling the beating heart
Feeling the soft hand navigating through places untouched
I do sense the smell that I knew and never left
Infinite thinking of you next to me

The Story Goes On

Once again I feel the silence around me
The room is already dark
I am guessing no one is around
Unforgettable fares coming into my mind
I see my immense sea, my vast sea and I sing
Sing the story of a past life
I feel the soft breeze caress my face
That breeze sounds like a violin
Keeping tune with my singing
The story goes on
The singing is always about love and tears
First time about everything
Talking, touching, kissing and sins
That was the package that I had to offer
Looking around I see your shadow
That comes and goes that fades away
Plunges back into the darkness of the deep
Isn't wise to think and pretend
Life goes on wrinkles and white hair
Will take over the youth that once was
I continue to sing hoping someday to return
From this voyage of dreams

Not Responsible Youth

New day is born, people walk around searching
The city lights are off, the morning is still cold
I got to find out about the news I heard last night
I am searching for someone to talk about it
Keep walking thinking what to do
Isn't a game this time is real no doubt about it
I am the only one responsible no excuses
Too young for what I am searching
The crowd looks strangely shaking their heads
I see what I am looking for
She is far coming close to show me
A fake smile on the baby angel face
I look it is real it shows she is a mom to be
Not responsible youth
What games we play will be remembered forever
I fall stay on the ground for awhile
Can't believe what I am seeing I the father
Hope it is a dream I got to awake keep looking
It will be a difficult reality to accept too young for it
That fake smile is talking seriously like a lady
Don't worry I will give you no problem Not responsible youth
I will remember the game that we played
We lied about the age, we lied about the love
I got to stand up can't let her be alone
A flower will born because of the game we played
I will be with her for eternity.

Alone I Am Not

As the wind blows through the gaps of the windows
My blood flows slowly into my brain
Tonight alone in my cabin
Can't warm the excitement of my body
As if by force of habit
The bar down the street coming to mind
Isn't close by I got to drive for awhile
But for sure I will find who will keep me warm
Inside I am the drink is ready
The voices in the air too familiar to stare
My name was mentioned still talking
The two girls in the corner send me a smile
I remember can't forget the countless hours
Alone I am not for the night coming
I plead for one to stay and keep me warm
The time has come the caring caresses shown
To let her feel my body
To the cold cabin on the mountain
Alone I am not I will remember the bar
Few drinks to start and a woman to finish.

The Transvestite

It isn't as easy it looks
Day after day the same walk of sins
With shiny shoes and six inch heels
Isn't easy to find the right hair
That will help me commit the sin
Cars stopping cars going by
Someone's got to pay for my body
Tears of regret coming down my eyes
When for few dollars I sell my body
I sell love in the middle of the street
For ten minutes of smiles and a caress
What does this dress hide a women or a man
I too don't understand
Deep into the night the sidewalk is mine
Few times I stop put my hands up high
Why me God ~Am I woman or a guy
I sell love in the middle of the street
Where people look to get some heat
The money that I get is money of sin
My heart aches I am not thrilled
I pray sometimes let me die
This isn't the life that let me by
The night is over the sun arises
Is time for me to leave the site
I walk home alone feeling shamed and tired
Go wash away the sins that I committed all night.

Running for Happiness

How many miles we ran together
Sunny days and deep rain
We were kids then looking for adventure
Reaching the forest trying to be alone
We had some laughs we had some regrets
It was a normal story for kids like us
We suffered in the way of young hearts
Looking for glory or something new in our dreams
Running for happiness
And praying into the deep of the night
To find faith in each mile
We were not afraid into the deep forest
Alone to embrace the silent surroundings
Sad it was when the daybreak called for reality
Going back to the city where we started to sin
We are not kids now good times gone by
Can't stay indifferent to life and its surroundings
If we sin we got to pay with our hearts and our minds
So sad to look around stop running
And say good bye to the happiness that was our life.

My House in Winter Time

The snow coming down I can see from my windows
The crystal flakes pile up on the ground
For hours I watch the sky
Seeing birds here and there flying
Looking for a meal left behind
I hear a dog barking playing around
He too enjoys the snow coming down
My house in winter time
Talks to me making strange sounds
Advises me the snow is getting high
Sometimes my tractor shows off to life
It is the only way to clean the frozen surroundings
Somewhere in the woods the noise is loud
Chainsaw and trees falling giving happy sounds
My house in the winter time is a castle
With me as king telling stories of past
Wife and kids and the smell of smoke
From the old wood burner
Waiting for that day for the snow to fade away
For now the cold snow will be my companion
This is my house in winter time.

You my Ghost

Not long ago your beauty was following me around
The perfume of your body keeping me awake at night
The sweat keeping clear our minds
To the morning when the sun starts to shine
You my ghost, memories never die
Feeling your breath through my spine
Even now that you are gone for awhile
Your image appears on my wall at night
Few times I was scared but not now
Lay in bed looking around we discuss
The happiness of our future that will never come
You my best friend now
Love, caresses are things of the past
We can talk about it without interacting with our bodies
Some nights it is a torment that never ends
Some night tears turn to laughs and we play around
You my ghost that keeps me company
That guides me through inner city wilds
I believe in you, the care that you give
Will always follow me into eternity.

The Upper Room

I hear you crying, I hear you sobbing for awhile
The story is always the same you think are ugly
Complexity of low self-esteem is the reason
The upper room is your shelter
Windows and door shut for eternity
No reason to let you be what you are
Few pimples showing on the beautiful skin
Makes you think you have sinned
Your age is young the woman in you has far to come
The silky long hair braided as a school girl
Changes are near no sobbing stop crying
Open the doors and windows
The Upper room returns to shine
Sun rain snow and wind keep you company
Leave the silky long hair flying
No creams and eye lashes needed
No glasses to cover the blue eyes
Tell me now who is the most beautiful around
Forget the problems that you had
Today is a new day go out into the city
Put on tight jeans like a star from a movie set
Laugh at the world no more tears and hiding
Leave the young age as you are
The upper room will always be your shelter
Where dreams in time will turn to reality.

Unrestful Night

Lie down in cold sheets my bed full of thorny
Memories of a one night stand visions of unrest
A number obscure my thoughts
From a game that I have been playing for awhile
It's different now the feeling succumb my heart
I got to be strong how many one night stands she went through
Can't close my eyes the image is next to me
The cold sheets the thorns penetrating my body
Relief is on the way if the number I call
I got to swear to forget that body to forget the sin
I don't want to call knowing I can't sleep I miss the smell
In the air the necessity to have her next to me
Torments my heart tears coming down my cheeks
Soaking the pillow sobbing talking words in the air
This will be a long sleepless night
Waiting for daylight hoping to forget
Looking at the white sheets I get lost
The solitude is my friend in this unrestful night
The images don't want leave my thoughts
The anger explodes my heart
One more tear into the soaked pillow
I still sobbing into a thousand words
Alone under the cold sheets.

Talking Simplicit

It was very simple to start a conversation
The way the debate started wasn't so intense
People around me would have preferred an evasion
This was me no one's fault
My friends if you don't want to listen go away
Talking Simplicity is my forte'
Dirty words flowing through my mind
Never make them the talk of the town
I listen to myself looking around
The faces of the crowd tell me it is time
The pain, the tears, printed on tiring faces
The hearts beating ready to explode
My speech on life wasn't pre-printed
Words were spoken no college degree involved
Happiness was the subject
Talking simplicity was my intent
Time went by fast two hours of talking
The looks were lost into evaporated air
I started to realize that no one gave a damn
My speech softened on words with no meaning
I too vanish into the evaporated air.

I am the Soldier

Where the sun goes to die at the end of the day
Where the wind goes to rest tired of blowing
The war machine stops singing words of terror
Memory of the past invading my thoughts
The temporary silence echoes my love
I am the soldier far from the lustful nights
I haven't forgotten sins committed
Closing my eyes dreaming of touching you
As sunset carried your words
I am the Soldier
With a story to tell
When time has come back from hell
Enemies and love the two main subjects
Day after day I got to wait
Fear for my woman making mistakes
The enemy taking my thoughts at sunrise
Get dutifully in the line to survive
Amid utter confusion I am alive
The story will be the same
I am the soldier back from war
The only thing I know, is my home

I Live for Her

I do not remember how she entered
Since then she is still here
The vibrant way of moving
Makes grey days sunny
I live for her
Isn't a burden don't be jealous
She belongs to all who need her
She can be that someone in the bedroom
To fulfill the emptiness of the lonely nights
I live for her
She is the muse that invades my body
Sweet and sensual she stuns without hurting
No traveling just suffering within the four walls
It is painful live in the hotel
Where pleasure is supreme in the vortex
Through my voice the melodic sayings produce love
I live for her
It is written on my face, my eyes illuminated
No limit for a harsh tomorrow
No conquest from protagonist that comes and goes
The music is the same a few murmuring and counting the money
I have no way out
I truly never betray her because she gives me the rest
The freedom is there, but not life
She is unique I will live for her.

Vacationing

Here in this paradise where the sea shines
And the wind howls
On the old terrace beside the gulf of Guilt
I admire a young man embracing a young girl
Still tears coming down the smooth skin
Making no sound only words whispering
Like a song saying I love you
It is a chain reaction that heats the blood
I am uninvited but I see the veins
The hot blood traveling in a fast tempo
Illuminating the old terrace
Where a dim light shows three shadows in the night
I felt the pain in the whispered words
The moon just emerging from behind a cloud
Seemed sweeter on him smiling
Giving light to the green eyes full of tears
Mixing with the salty sea drowning
The power of the opera
Where every drama is a true story
I will be someone who lived that drama
Never forget the words that confused my thoughts
So everything makes sense
Yes this was a story that ended
I didn't think much of the future
On the contrary I felt uninvited
Continued my vacationing

Nightingales on my Windowsill

Don't stop now my little bird keep singing
I don't understand what you are trying to say
I don't rush you away even if it is early in the morning
You awake me before the sun rises
Maybe I know why you sing on my windowsill
Tell me that it is a new day
You are welcome the new born dawn
Making sure that I awake and am lucky to be alive
I look at you from my glass window
You beautiful nightingale so tiny give me a smile
Your mission is accomplished you fly away
Your next stop is a far away branch full of green leaves
Where another nightingale waits for your love
And spending the day together in search of food
Playing flying through the sky drinking when you thirst
Back on making love nothing to worry about
Now two nightingales resting on my windowsill
Flying like gypsies over my head
I call you over, trying to talk to be close to me
Too far into the sky to hear my call
Keep fluttering and saying good morning to spring
I will wait for you the next day on my windowsill
Awaking from your singing
Be out and running into the meadow
Fluttering and be curious about this new day
And never die but continuing to listen to your singing.

Accused

The word all over town has spread
I am wanted by the ladies
Knowing that I will be captured sooner or later
The crime that I committed is in the daily news
That I steal hearts and then abuse
Word of love is the weapon I use
And now I stand in front of you accused
Before you pass a sentence I said
Hear my story it is only about love
I give your lady my heart my body and soul
I really thought that I was in love with you
Your lady should not cry for times well spent
It will be a memory of the past in your heart
For that and only that I am guilty
I will take my sentence with an open heart
Before the story ends and I will be sentenced
I want to say to you all
Give me a chance and I will do it again
My body is made for sharing till the end
So people of the jury tell me my sentence
I will not cry to spend the rest of my life alone
Because the only thing I am guilty is love.

The Way I See Things

Well the end has come
For better or worse I spoke my mind
The way I see things is complete
Just waiting to be criticized
It wasn't easy it took me awhile
To put all the thoughts together and finalize
Time well-spent on this writing
Many waking nights thinking aloud
I am not a poet just an ordinary guy
That likes to write and visualize
The Way I see things is a part of life
Lived every day to not surprise
Maybe a few will be offended a few will be proud
To read about themselves in a rhyme
Here in New Hampshire where life is sublime
The way to express thoughts is to write.

www.ingramcontent.com/pod-product-compliance
Lightning Source LLC
LaVergne TN
LVHW092051060526
838201LV00047B/1338